Aye-Aye
An Evil Omen

by Miriam Aronin

Consultant: Eleanor Sterling, Ph.D.
Director, Center for Biodiversity and Conservation
American Museum of Natural History

BEARPORT
PUBLISHING

New York, New York

Credits

Cover and Title Page, © David Haring/Oxford Scientific Films/Photolibrary; TOC, © A & J Visage/ Alamy; 4–5, © Frans Lanting/Minden Pictures; 6T, © Cyril Ruoso/JH Editorial/Minden Pictures; 6B, © Kevin Frey; 8, © New York Public Library; 9, © Frans Lanting/Minden Pictures; 9TL, © Pete Oxford/Nature Picture Library; 9BR, © Nick Garbutt/npl/Minden Pictures; 10, © Lynn M. Stone/ Nature Picture Library; 11, © Elizabeth Bomford/ardea.com; 12L, © Pete Oxford/Nature Picture Library; 12R, © Nick Garbutt/npl/Minden Pictures; 13, © Olivier Langrand/Peter Arnold Inc.; 14, © Frans Lanting/Minden Pictures; 15, © David Haring/Oxford Scientific Films/Photolibrary; 16, © A & J Visage/Alamy; 17L, © A & J Visage/Alamy; 17R, © Rhett A. Butler/wildmadagascar.org; 18L, © A & J Visage/Alamy; 18R, © Chris Hellier/Chris Hellier Photography; 19, © David Haring/OSF/Animals Animals-Earth Scenes; 20, © A & J Visage/Alamy; 21T, © Barrie Britton/Nature Picture Library; 21B, © A & J Visage/Alamy; 22, © Lemur Conservation Foundation; 23, © Frans Lanting/Minden Pictures; 24, © Bristol Zoo/Press Association/AP Images; 25, © David Haring/Oxford Scientific Films/ Photolibrary; 26–27, © David Haring/Oxford Scientific Films/Photolibrary; 28, © Frans Lanting/ Minden Pictures; 29T, © Pete Oxford/Minden Pictures; 29B, © Gerald Cubitt/BIOS/Peter Arnold Inc.; 32, © DANI/JESKE/Animals Animals-Earth Scenes.

Publisher: Kenn Goin
Editorial Director: Adam Siegel
Creative Director: Spencer Brinker
Original Design: Dawn Beard Creative
Photo Researcher: Jennifer Bright

Library of Congress Cataloging-in-Publication Data

Aronin, Miriam.
  Aye-aye : an evil omen / by Miriam Aronin.
     p. cm. — (Uncommon animals)
  Includes bibliographical references and index.
  ISBN-13: 978-1-59716-731-4 (library binding)
  ISBN-10: 1-59716-731-2 (library binding)
  1. Aye-aye—Juvenile literature. I. Title.

QL737.P935A76 2009
599.8'3—dc22
                            2008015387

For more information, write to Bearport Publishing Company, Inc., 101 Fifth Avenue, Suite 6R, New York, New York 10003. Printed in the United States of America.

10 9 8 7 6 5 4 3 2 1

Contents

A Surprise in the Dark

It was evening in northeastern Madagascar. Eleanor Sterling and Alison Jolly had been traveling through the **rain forest** all day. The two American scientists were looking for monkey-like animals called **lemurs**. Suddenly, they saw something move.

About 60 kinds of lemurs live in Madagascar. Lemurs exist in the wild only in Madagascar and nearby islands.

A shadowy figure ran across a palm tree branch and grabbed a coconut. Alison turned on her head lamp. The women saw a small animal with black-and-silver fur and huge shining eyes.

The strange creature chewed a hole in the coconut. Then it stuck a long bony finger inside and started pulling out some of the white fruit. Eleanor and Alison knew that only one type of lemur ate like that—the **rare** aye-aye (EYE-eye)!

The aye-aye is about the size of a house cat.

Meet the Scientists

Biologists Eleanor Sterling and Alison Jolly had met up in Madagascar in the late 1980s. Both had come to the island to study its uncommon animals. Many of these creatures, including aye-ayes, live nowhere else in the world. Alison had been studying wildlife in Madagascar since 1963, but Eleanor had just started her studies.

Alison Jolly (right) has studied many different kinds of lemurs, including the ring-tailed lemur.

Eleanor Sterling focused her studies on one kind of lemur—the aye-aye.

Eleanor first learned about aye-ayes and other types of lemurs in college. She remembered how her teacher had "danced across the stage **mimicking** a lemur jumping from tree to tree."

Eleanor became very curious about these unusual creatures. So she traveled to Madagascar to learn more about them, especially the aye-aye.

Aye-Ayes in the Wild

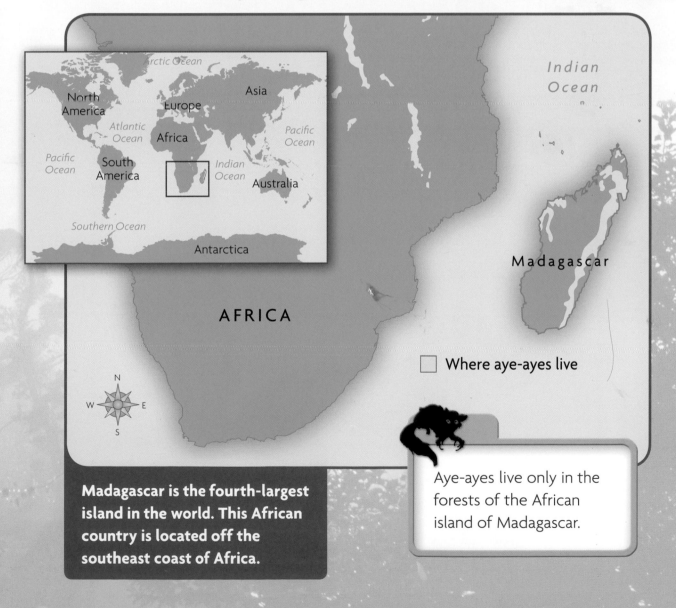

Where aye-ayes live

Madagascar is the fourth-largest island in the world. This African country is located off the southeast coast of Africa.

Aye-ayes live only in the forests of the African island of Madagascar.

A Very Odd Animal

Eleanor began the first long-term study of aye-ayes in the wild. Yet she was not the first person to study them. Scientists first saw the odd-looking creature in the late 1700s. At the time, however, they weren't even sure what kind of animal it was.

The aye-aye looks like a combination of different creatures. It has a furry tail like a fox and big ears like a bat. It has large front teeth, and it lives in trees. At first, scientists mistakenly thought it was a kind of squirrel.

An early drawing of an aye-aye

Scientists didn't figure out that the aye-aye is a type of lemur until the mid-1800s. The word "lemur" comes from the Latin word for "ghost." Explorers called the animals they saw lemurs because of their ghostly howls and big glowing eyes.

mongoose lemur

black lemur

Lemurs are animals in the **primate** group. Other primates include monkeys, gorillas, orangutans, and humans.

black-and-white ruffed lemur

An Evil Omen

Unfortunately, the aye-aye's odd looks have caused many people in Madagascar to fear it. Some people think that the animal is an evil **omen**. They believe that if someone sees a very small aye-aye, a child will soon die. If someone sees a larger aye-aye, they think an adult will die.

Not everyone in Madagascar fears the aye-aye. In an area of southeastern Madagascar, people believe that the aye-aye is a sign of good luck.

For hundreds of years, people killed aye-ayes because they thought it would stop the animals from causing harm. Scientists who heard stories about aye-ayes wanted to learn more about them. Yet the aye-aye **population** was so small that it was hard to find and study this mysterious creature.

Aye-ayes sometimes eat farm crops such as coconuts, mangoes, and sugarcane. Some farmers kill or drive away the lemurs to protect their food.

Almost Extinct

Scientists had such a hard time finding aye-ayes that they declared the animal **extinct** in 1935. About 20 years later, however, aye-ayes were discovered in several places in Madagascar. To protect these rare creatures, scientists moved nine aye-ayes to a small **reserve**. They hoped the animals could live safely and **mate** there.

In 1966, nine aye-ayes were placed in a reserve on the tiny African island of Nosy Mangabe.

An aye-aye on Nosy Mangabe

Scientists wanted to do more to help the aye-aye. Yet they knew so little about it. What could they do? Eleanor Sterling decided to find out. In the 1980s, she traveled to Madagascar to learn more about this misunderstood creature.

In the 1950s, people began chopping down Madagascar's trees more than ever before. The trees were cut down for wood and to make room for farms. Luckily, aye-ayes can live in rain forests even after many of the trees have been removed.

Trees used to cover this area of Madagascar.

Tough to Track

Eleanor had to work hard to find aye-ayes to study. The animals are **nocturnal**, so they sleep during the day. Each afternoon, Eleanor would search for an aye-aye sleeping in a tree. When she found one, she waited until the small animal woke up in the evening. Then she followed it until sunrise.

Aye-ayes sleep high in trees, in nests built from leafy branches.

At night, aye-ayes move quickly through the rain forest **canopy**. Eleanor followed on the ground in the dark, carrying headphones, binoculars, and other equipment. "They almost never stop to rest. I was basically walking the whole night," she said.

In one night, an aye-aye can travel almost three miles (5 km). Their big eyes help them see so that they can make their way through the dark.

Like No Other Primate

As Eleanor tracked and studied aye-ayes, she was able to see up close how different they are from other primates, such as gorillas and orangutans. For example, most primates have short, flat nails that cover the tops of their fingers and toes. The aye-aye, however, has long, thin claws that curve down from most of its fingers and toes.

The long, sharp claws of an aye-aye

There are more differences, too. The aye-aye's front teeth never stop growing. Such teeth are common in **rodents** like mice and beavers but not among primates.

The aye-aye also has an extra eyelid on each eye. According to Eleanor, the extra eyelid protects its eyes "when it is **gnawing** wood and bits are flying everywhere."

Aye-ayes use their long teeth to gnaw into fruits, nuts, and wood.

This fruit was chewed by an aye-aye.

A Special Finger

Aye-ayes have another very unusual **feature**. They have an extra-thin third finger on each hand. It is very **flexible**. The aye-aye can bend it in all directions. They can even bend their finger back against their hand.

The aye-aye's third finger is much thinner than the other fingers on its hand.

Eleanor and Alison saw how this special finger helps the aye-aye survive. They watched it use its third finger to scoop food from nuts. The finger also helps the aye-aye to eat quickly. The animal can move its third finger between its mouth and its food three times every second.

An aye-aye using its third finger to get food out of an egg

The aye-aye uses its extra-thin third finger like a **tool** to help it get food.

Finding Food

Aye-ayes also use their extra-thin finger to find insect **larvae**. The larvae live inside the hollow parts of trees. Ayes-ayes tap trees and branches with their special finger. When they hear a hollow sound, they gnaw the wood away. They then reach inside the hole with their third finger, pull out the larvae, and eat them.

Ayes-ayes leave unique marks on trees where they have found insect larvae.

Eleanor saw this behavior many times. "Aye-ayes eat really big, chunky larvae just like a child eating an ice cream cone," she said. "The insect's insides . . . drip down the aye-aye's fingers, so the animal runs its tongue around its hand to lick the juicy parts up fast."

An aye-aye hunting for larvae

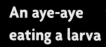
An aye-aye eating a larva

Learning from Aye-Ayes

After two years of hard work, Eleanor finished her research. She used what she had learned to update school books with information about the aye-aye for students and teachers in Madagascar. If people learn more about the animal, perhaps they will look for more ways to protect it.

Ny Aiay Ako

Written by Alison Jolly
Illustrated by Deborah Ross
Malagasy text by
Hantanirina Rasamimanana

Alison Jolly wrote the children's book *Ako the Aye-Aye* to help children in Madagascar and around the world learn about aye-ayes. It is written in both English and Malagasy, two of the official languages of Madagascar.

Eleanor's efforts to teach people about aye-ayes are also important to science. Researchers can learn a lot from these animals. For example, some biologists are studying how aye-ayes see colors. The results may help scientists better understand how other animals see.

Scientists were surprised to learn that aye-ayes see in color. They once thought that since aye-ayes are awake only at night, they would not need color vision.

New Babies

Other researchers are working on a different way to help aye-ayes. They have set up programs to **breed** the animal in **captivity**. If wild aye-ayes become extinct, then the aye-ayes born in zoos can be released into Madagascar's rain forests.

This baby aye-aye was born at the Bristol Zoo in England.

In 1992, the first aye-aye was born in captivity. The baby was born in North Carolina at Duke University's Lemur Center. Since then, at least 15 more aye-ayes have been born there.

An aye-aye born at Duke University

Today, more than 35 **captive** aye-ayes live in the United States, England, France, Japan, and Madagascar.

The Future for Aye-Ayes

Counting aye-ayes in captivity is easy. Counting them in the wild is difficult. Eleanor said, "Aye-ayes live in more places in Madagascar than we thought. But we still don't know exactly how many live in any one place."

Today, aye-ayes are still losing some of their **habitat** to farming and logging. Some people still believe aye-ayes are an evil omen and continue to kill them.

However, there are hopeful signs. The government of Madagascar wants to triple the size of protected forest areas where aye-ayes can live. Villagers will work with the government and **conservation** groups to decide where and how the forests will be saved. With people's help, this rare animal will have the bright future it deserves.

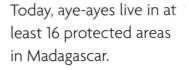

Today, aye-ayes live in at least 16 protected areas in Madagascar.

Aye-Aye Facts

The aye-aye is a member of the primate family, like chimpanzees, apes, and humans. It has large eyes and ears and a very thin third finger. Here are some other facts about this uncommon animal.

Weight	**males:** 5.9 pounds (2.7 kg) **females:** 5.5 pounds (2.5 kg)
Length	**males:** 12.6 inches (32 cm) long, plus a tail that is about the same length **females:** 12 inches (30 cm) long, plus a tail that is about the same length
Food	insect larvae, nuts, fruit, fungi, seeds, nectar
Life Span	about 25 years in captivity; unknown in the wild
Habitat	the forests of Madagascar
Population	unknown

More Uncommon Animals

The aye-aye is one kind of uncommon animal in Madagascar. Many other unusual animals also live there.

Fossa

- The fossa looks like a large cat but it is related to the mongoose.
- Fossas are the top hunters living in Madagascar. They hunt and eat lemurs, wild pigs, mice, and snakes.
- Many people in Madagascar fear fossas and kill them. Fossas are now in danger of becoming extinct.
- As few as 2,500 fossas live in the forests of Madagascar.

Pygmy Mouse Lemur

- The pygmy mouse lemur is the smallest primate in the world. Its head and body together are less than 2.5 inches (6 cm) long, with a tail about 4.75 inches (12 cm) long.
- Pygmy mouse lemurs weigh 1 ounce (28 g), about the weight of 10 pennies.
- They live in trees in Madagascar's dry forests.
- Like aye-ayes, pygmy mouse lemurs are nocturnal.
- Scientists know very little about these uncommon animals. Their life span is unknown.
- They are believed to eat fruit, flowers, and insects.

Glossary

biologists (bye-OL-uh-jists) scientists who study animals or plants

breed (BREED) to have young

canopy (KAN-uh-pee) the top layer of leaves and branches covering a forest

captive (KAP-tiv) held so one cannot escape

captivity (kap-TIV-uh-*tee*) a place where an animal lives that is not its natural home and where it cannot travel freely

conservation (*kon*-sur-VAY-shuhn) the protection of wildlife and nature

extinct (ek-STINGKT) when a kind of plant or animal has died out; no more of its kind is living anywhere in the world

feature (FEE-chur) an important part or quality of something

flexible (FLEK-suh-buhl) able to bend easily

gnawing (NAW-ing) biting or chewing over and over

habitat (HAB-uh-*tat*) a place in nature where plants or animals normally live

larvae (LAR-vee) young insects, which look like worms and do not yet have wings

lemurs (LEE-murz) furry animals that usually have long tails and large eyes; they are in the primate family and live mainly in Madagascar

mate (MAYT) to come together to have young

mimicking (MIM-ik-ing) copying or imitating

nocturnal (nok-TUR-nuhl) active only at night

omen (OH-muhn) a sign or warning of good or bad events in the future

population (*pop*-yuh-LAY-shuhn) the total number of a kind of animal living in a place

primate (PRYE-mate) an animal in the family that includes humans, monkeys, apes, and lemurs

rain forest (RAYN FOR-ist) a warm, wet place where it rains very often and where lots of trees and plants grow

rare (RAIR) not often found or seen

reserve (ri-SURV) an area of land set aside as a safe place for plants and animals to live

rodents (ROHD-uhnts) small mammals with long front teeth, such as mice, rats, rabbits, and beavers

tool (TOOL) an object that is used to do a job

Bibliography

American Museum of Natural History. "The Uncommon Aye-Aye: An Interview with Eleanor Sterling" (2004).
amnh.org/sciencebulletins/bio/f/lemurs.20060401/essays/81_1.php

Arizona State University. "Color Night Vision in the Aye-Aye, a Most Unusual Primate," *ScienceDaily* (September 12, 2007).
www.sciencedaily.com/releases/2007/09/070904114535.htm

Durrell, Gerald. *The Aye-Aye and I: A Rescue Mission in Madagascar.* New York: Touchstone (1992).

Gron, K. J. "Primate Factsheets: Aye-aye (*Daubentonia madagascariensis*) Taxonomy, Morphology, & Ecology," *Primate Info Net* (July 27, 2007).
pin.primate.wisc.edu/factsheets/entry/aye-aye

Jolly, Alison. "Madagascar's Lemurs: On the Edge of Survival," *National Geographic*, Vol. 174, No. 2 (August 1988).

Read More

Blauer, Ettagale, and Jason Lauré. *Madagascar (Enchantment of the World).* New York: Children's Press (2000).

Corwin, Jeff. *Into Wild Madagascar.* San Diego, CA: Blackbirch Press (2004).

Lasky, Kathryn. *Shadows in the Dawn: The Lemurs of Madagascar.* San Diego, CA: Harcourt (1998).

Oluonye, Mary N. *Madagascar.* Minneapolis, MN: Carolrhoda Books (2000).

Learn More Online

To learn more about aye-ayes, visit
www.bearportpublishing.com/UncommonAnimals

Index

About the Author

Miriam Aronin is a writer and editor. She also enjoys reading, knitting, and visiting unusual animals at the zoo.